(An imprint of Clever Fox Publishing Pvt. Ltd.)

A note from the author :

The Planet Talks" takes readers on a captivating adventure through the vastness of space, where a young explorer finds himself in a remarkable encounter with planets that can speak. In this unique interstellar journey, readers will come across many thought-provoking explorations on planets and connect themselves with their emotions.

© Books Mantra

All rights reserved. No part of this book may be reproduced or transmitted in any form by any means, electronic or mechanical, including photocopying and recording, or by any information storage and retrieval system except as may be expressly permitted in writing by the publisher.

(An imprint of Clever Fox Publishing Pvt. Ltd.)

Books Mantra 2024
8 Sarva Space, 2nd Floor, SBI Bank Building,
Harinagara Cross Konankunte Post,
Anjanapura Main Rd, Bengaluru,
Karnataka 560062
www.booksmantra.com

THE PLANET TALKS

Written by

RAYA

Illustrated by

SAMUEL

It was pitch dark when I opened my eyes and found myself floating. Any guesses where I would be?

Yes! I was in space. Even though I was wearing my white space gear, I was freezing. I could feel the weight of the oxygen cylinder connected to my space gear.

The Earth asked me, "What's the current talk going on among the humans?" I said, "The humans are having a talk about moving to another planet".

The Earth was terrified to hear that news and said "Why so? Am I not meeting their needs?"

"Yes you are," I said. Earth in a worried tone said, "You people dump trash on me, pollute my water resources, and destroy my forest land, I never hated you people, and in return, I tried to be more kind and nice to you all". "So only we call you MOTHER EARTH, who shows endless love to us ", I said with gratitude.

I pacified the Earth with my words and gave the info that as a part of research, many countries are sending their space shuttle to Mars and other planets to see if they are fit for human life. Even my teacher told us maybe in three decades people may travel to Mars as we were traveling in airplanes to other countries.

The Earth became sadder and sadder as I talked. I could sense its feeling and told the Earth, "You don't get upset! They are just doing research and you are always special to us". I couldn't see the sad face of Earth more so I bid 'Goodbye' and moved to meet other planets.

From nowhere I heard a "Hello", that was none other than the 'Rusty Red Mars'. It looks so vibrant but it's too cold when I stood next to him. Mars was so kind and asked about my well-being and journey in exploring space.

"Hello"

I told him about the conversation that happened between Earth and me. It was happy since humans were sending spaceships and doing research to make life in space for humans. It was also sad because its friend Earth was upset about this matter.

Mars said, "Hey, my little friend can you accompany me to meet my friend Earth? "Then we both met Earth. Mars said, "My dear friend Earth, no one's existence can harm you or make your fame go less, so light up and you be yourself". I could see a little brim of a smile on Earth's face.

Mars added, "You are always unique and have everything to make human life easy and in my and others' case the humans had to do research to make us fit for their lives, but you are created for humans!" This brought more energy and power to Earth.

It was so good to see such a healthy conversation happening between them. I felt how nice and kind these planets are to each other, we humans fight for small and silly things. Finally, I bid 'Goodbye' to both and started to move.

Suddenly, I heard an alarm sound, my dream was shattered, I woke up and checked the time. It was almost time to get ready for school! Then I rushed.

When I sat at my breakfast table, the hot steaming idlis reminded me of the moons of the planets, and the dots on them were similar to the craters.
I relished each bite of my breakfast thinking about my dream and went to school happily and told my dream to my friends and our teacher. Everybody enjoyed my dream the same way I did.

Colour me

www.ingramcontent.com/pod-product-compliance
Lightning Source LLC
LaVergne TN
LVHW070940070526
838199LV00039B/727